Who'll Be President?

Happy House

About Wise & Wide

- A systematic 6-level English reading program based on Lexile® measures
- Diverse and interesting topics chosen from the elementary curriculums of Korea and English speaking western countries
- Well-written books in various forms including fiction stories, descriptive texts, and classics retold
- The informative but original fiction stories grab your interest, leading to the easy and clear understanding of the educational content.
- Improve thinking skills with solid after-reading activities at all levels of the series.

Wise & Wide is a 6-level English reading program that consists of 60 books and each level is systematically divided by Lexile® measures. The Lexile® Framework for Reading is the most popular reading measuring system in American formal education curriculums and many English programs. Over 20 out of 50 states in the U.S. mark Lexile® measures directly on students' final report cards and over 300 well-known publishers adopt and use Lexile® measures.

Experience many kinds of readings written by professional writers from the U.S. and England. They used interesting topics that were carefully chosen after analyzing elementary curriculums from around the world including Korea, the U.S., England, and Australia among many others. Comprehensive after-reading activities including graphic organizers, speaking tasks, and After-reading Tests are ready for you.

Levels in the series and their corresponding Lexile® measures

Level	Lexile® measures	U.S. Grade
Level 1	Below 200L	Pre K - K
Level 2	190L - 400L	Lower Grade 1
Level 3	350L - 530L	Upper Grade 1
Level 4	420L - 650L	Grade 2
Level 5	520L - 940L	Grade 3 - 4
Level 6	830L - 1070L	Grade 5 - 6

* Smart Readers: Wise & Wide level 1 is applicable to the preschool level in the U.S.

* The source of the relationship between Lexile® measures and U.S. school grades: CCSS(Common Core State Standards) FOR ENGLISH LANGUAGE ARTS, APPENDIX A (2012, which is used by 45 states in the U.S.)

Topic List

	Level 1	Level 2	Level 3	Level 4	Level 5	Level 6
Book 1	Science>Biology: The hibernation of animals Story	Science>Biology: Living and nonliving things Story	Science>Biology> Animals & the Environment: Sea otters Story	Environment> Living with nature: The diver & the persimmon tree Story	Science>Biology> Animal: Amazing animals of the Amazon Story	Science>Biology: Germs, transmitted diseases Story
Book 2	Literature> World classics: Aesop's fables Story	Literature> Traditional fairy tale: Old tales about stones Story	Social Studies> Economy: To run a business to make and save money Story	Science>Biology> Plants: Photosynthesis Story	Science>Earth science: Earth's layers, earthquakes, volcanoes, and earth's atmosphere Report	Mathematics> Sequence: The golden ratio & the Fibonacci sequence Story
Book 3	Science>Physics: How shadows are formed Story	Literature> World classics: Peter Pan Story	Science>Scientific technology: Nanobots Story	Literature>Myths: World's creation stories Story	Literature> Legend: The story of King Arthur Story	Literature>Myths: Constellation myths Story
Book 4	Literature> Traditional literature: The Talmud Story	Science>Biology> Animal: Polar bears Story	Science>Biology> Animal: Mountain gorillas Story	Social Studies> Cultural anthropology: Amazing ancient cultures of the world Story	Science> Earth science: Clouds and weather Story	Literature> Human & animals: The friendship between a girl and a horse Story
Book 5	Social Studies> Ethics: Rules in daily life Story	Science>Biology: The five senses Report	Social Studies> Cultural anthropology: Astonishing festivals Report	Art>Music: Stories from two operas Story	Social Studies> World culture & history: The Renaissance Story	Sports> Board sports: Surfing & snowboarding Story
Book 6	Social Studies> World geography & travel: Tourist attractions around the world Story	Science>Biology> Animal: Dinosaurs Story	Science> Astronomy: The solar system Story	Social Studies> People: Three great people who overcame hardships Story	Science>Scientific technology: The wonderful world of robots Report	Art>Music: Composers of the Romantic Era Report
Book 7	Science> Space science: The life of astronauts Report	Social Studies> Cultural anthropology: Mythological monsters from around the world Report	Mathematics> Elementary mathematics: Numbers, measurement, shapes and data Report	Science & Social Studies> Technology & culture: Inventions from around the world Report	Art>Works of art: Famous paintings Report	Social Studies> Human & animals: Animals in action for human Report
Book 8	Social Studies> Cultural anthropology: Various living cultures of the world Story	Art>Music: Instruments in the orchestra Story	Social Studies> Life safety: Learning and using outdoor survival skills Story	Social Studies> History: The California Gold Rush Report	Social Studies & Science> Psychology: Psychology in everyday life Story	Literature> World classics: The Merchant of Venice Story
Book 9	Social Studies> Jobs: Interviews about jobs Report	Science>Scientific technology: Developments in technology in different times Story	Social Studies> Politics>Election: Running for 3rd grade class president Story	Literature> World classics: Stories of Sherlock Holmes Story	Literature> World classics: Adrift in the Pacific Story	Social Studies> History & People: Great world leaders in history Report
Book 10	Literature>Traditional fairy tale: Eastern and Western folk tales on the same theme Story	Sports>Winter sports: Various aspects of some Winter Olympic sports Report	Literature> World classics: Short stories by O. Henry Story	Sports> Ball games: Various aspects of popular ball games Report	Social Studies> History: Famous events that changed world history Report	Art & Social Studies> Art: Stories about the creation, distribution, and preservation of paintings Report

* 10 books in each level will be published.

How to Use This Book

•Before Reading

You can easily find the topic and what kind of story you are about to read.

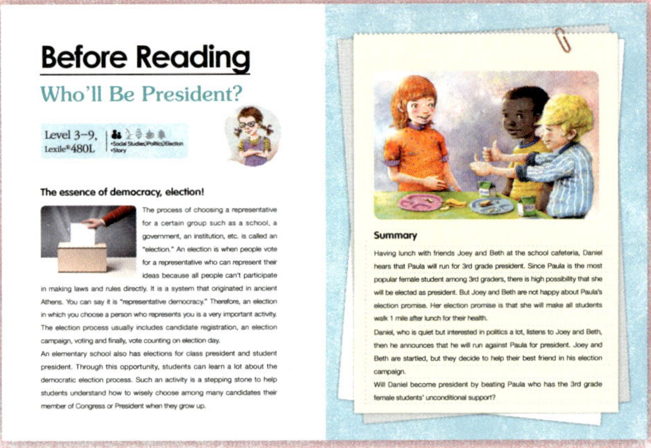

•The text

All the stories were written by professional writers from the U.S. and England, so you will read authentic and appropriate English sentences and expressions in every book in the series.

•Pop Quiz

Check out right away if you understand what you have just read by solving a pop quiz that checks your comprehension.

•Key Words

The key words and expressions on each page are listed for you to easily study them.

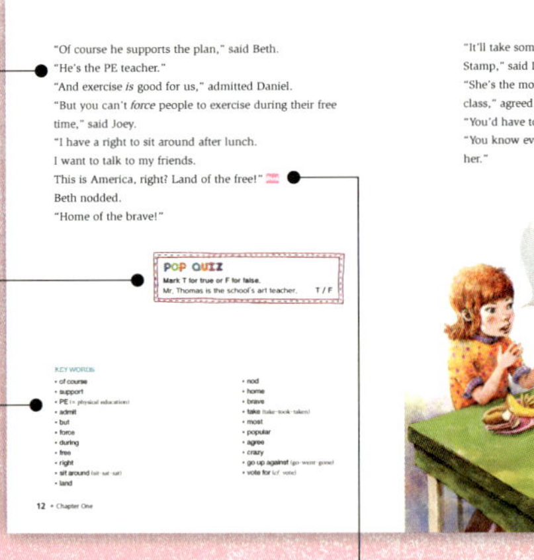

•Aha! Tips

Download free Korean explanations at *www.ihappyhouse.co.kr* for all of the sentences marked with "Aha!". These explain cultural, scientific, and economic knowledge or they deal with aspects of English such as grammatical structures or idiomatic expressions. There are lots of "Aha! Tips" to help you understand the text.

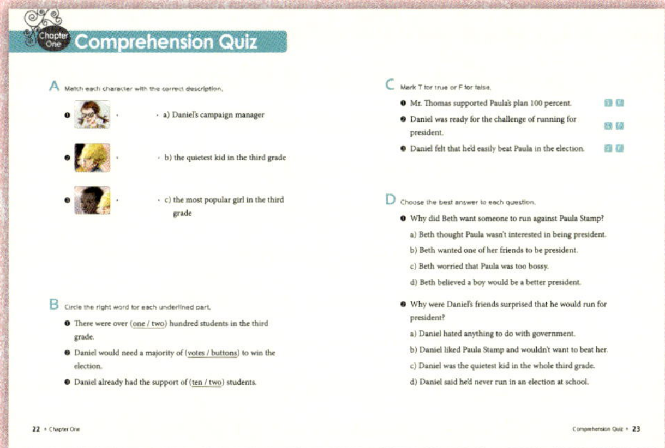

•Comprehension Quiz

After reading one chapter, solve various questions to find out if you fully understand the content.

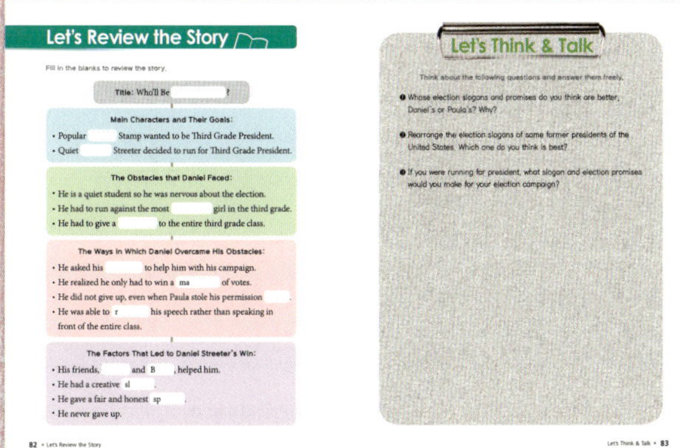

•Let's Review the Story /
•Let's Think & Talk

Fill in the blanks in the organizer to summarize the whole story. Express your own thinking and feelings about the story by answering the questions. You can build up logic and reasoning skills for your essay examinations in the future.

Appendix

Audio CD

In the CD audio book form, the texts are read vividly by American professional voice actors.
(MP3 files downloaded for free)

After-reading Test

Solve an additionally provided After-reading Test for each book.

The Korean translation, Answer Keys, a Word Quiz, a Word List, and Aha! Tips for each book

You can download them for free at *www.ihappyhouse.co.kr* or *www.darakwon.co.kr*

Before Reading

Who'll Be President?

The essence of democracy, election!

The process of choosing a representative for a certain group such as a school, a government, an institution, etc. is called an "election." An election is when people vote for a representative who can represent their ideas because all people can't participate in making laws and rules directly. It is a system that originated in ancient Athens. You can say it is "representative democracy." Therefore, an election in which you choose a person who represents you is a very important activity. The election process usually includes candidate registration, an election campaign, voting and finally, vote counting on election day.

An elementary school also has elections for class president and student president. Through this opportunity, students can learn a lot about the democratic election process. Such an activity is a stepping stone to help students understand how to wisely choose among many candidates their member of Congress or President when they grow up.

Summary

Having lunch with friends Joey and Beth at the school cafeteria, Daniel hears that Paula will run for 3rd grade president. Since Paula is the most popular female student among 3rd graders, there is high possibility that she will be elected as president. But Joey and Beth are not happy about Paula's election promise. Her election promise is that she will make all students walk 1 mile after lunch for their health.

Daniel, who is quiet but interested in politics a lot, listens to Joey and Beth, then he announces that he will run against Paula for president. Joey and Beth are startled, but they decide to help their best friend in his election campaign.

Will Daniel become president by beating Paula who has the 3rd grade female students' unconditional support?

Contents

Who'll Be President?

Who'll Be President?

Chapter One

Up for a Challenge

Daniel sat at the lunch table with his two best friends, Joey and Beth.

The school cafeteria buzzed with news.

The third grade class elections were just around the corner!

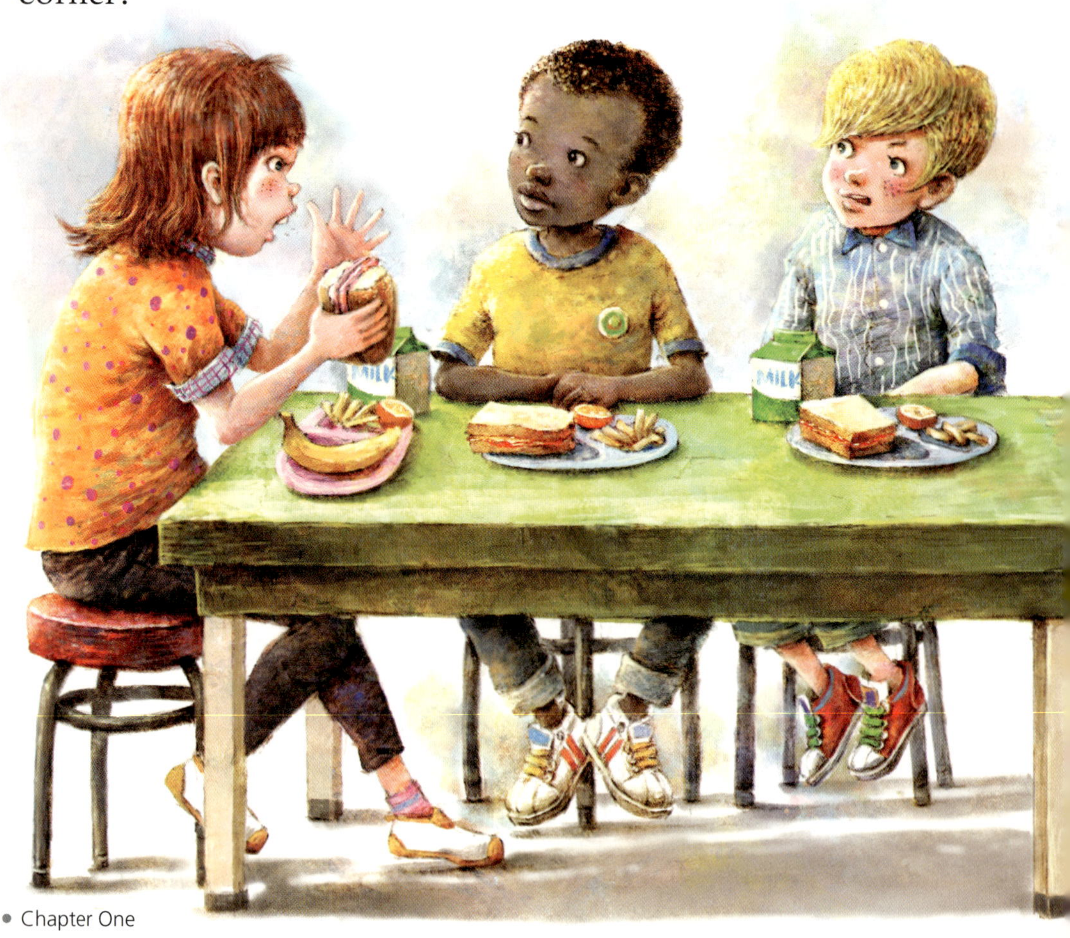

"Someone *has* to run against Paula," said Beth.

She chewed her bologna sandwich.

"We can't have her boss us around for an entire year!" Joey groaned.

"She'll make our lives miserable.

Did you hear about her latest idea?

She wants every single third grader to walk a mile after lunch.

She says exercise is good for us.

And Mr. Thomas is behind the plan 100 percent!"

▲ bologna

"Of course he supports the plan," said Beth.

"He's the PE teacher."

"And exercise *is* good for us," admitted Daniel.

"But you can't *force* people to exercise during their free time," said Joey.

"I have a right to sit around after lunch.

I want to talk to my friends.

This is America, right? Land of the free!" 

Beth nodded.

"Home of the brave!"

POP QUIZ

Mark T for true or F for false.

Mr. Thomas is the school's art teacher. T / F

KEY WORDS

- of course
- support
- **PE** (= physical education)
- admit
- but
- force
- during
- free
- right
- sit around (sit-sat-sat)
- land

- nod
- home
- brave
- take (take-took-taken)
- most
- popular
- agree
- crazy
- go up against (go-went-gone)
- vote for (*cf.* vote)

"It'll take someone really brave to run against Paula Stamp," said Daniel.

"She's the most popular girl in the entire third grade class," agreed Beth.

"You'd have to be crazy to go up against her," said Joey. "You know every girl in the third grade will vote for her."

It was true, Daniel thought.

Paula Stamp would be impossible to beat.

And yet, Daniel liked politics.

He thought he'd make a good president for his grade.

He was fair and a good listener.

He had lots of good ideas for third graders.

"I'm going to run for Third Grade President," said Daniel. Aha!

Beth dropped her banana. "You?"

Joey's milk dribbled down his chin. "Seriously?"

Daniel expected their reactions.

Sure, he was fair and a good listener.

He might even have lots of great ideas.

But Daniel Streeter was just about the *quietest* kid in the whole third grade.

Hardly anyone knew he existed.

Still, someone had to run against Paula.

KEY WORDS

- **think** (think-thought-thought)
- **impossible**
- **beat** (beat-beat-beaten)
- **and yet**
- **politics**
- **fair**
- **listener**
- **lots of**
- **drop**
- **dribble**
- **chin**
- **seriously**
- **expect**
- **reaction**
- **sure**
- **might + *Verb***
- **even**
- **just about**
- **quietest**
- **hardly**
- **anyone**
- **know** (know-knew-known)
- **exist**
- **still**

Daniel turned to his friends.

"I'm a little scared but I'm going to do it.

Will you help me?"

Beth sighed.

Daniel didn't have a chance of winning.

But Daniel was one of her best friends.

"Okay," she said.

"I'm in. But we have to get to work.

▲ a thumbs up gesture

We'll need a slogan and buttons and posters."

"I'm in, too," said Joey.

"You need a great campaign manager."

He made a thumbs up gesture to Beth and Daniel.

"We can do this!"

POP QUIZ
Who agreed to help Daniel with his campaign?
ⓐ Beth and Joey
ⓑ the majority of boys in the third grade

Daniel swallowed the last of his peanut butter and jelly sandwich.

Had he bitten off more than he could chew, running for Third Grade President?

There were over one hundred or so kids who made up the third grade. **Aha!**

It would be difficult to win over all of them.

But then Daniel smiled.

He didn't need the vote of *every* student.

He only needed a *majority* of the votes.

Fifty-five votes or so didn't seem like that much.

And he already had the three votes at his lunch table.

"Come on, guys," said Daniel.

"I need to tell our teacher that I'm throwing my hat in the ring." Aha!

"That's a funny thing to say," said Joey.

"You're not wearing a hat."

KEY WORDS

- **Come on!**
- **guys** (*cf.* guy)
- **throw one's hat in the ring**
  (throw-threw-thrown)
- **funny**
- **thing**
- **wear** (wear-wore-worn)

"It means I'm ready for a challenge," said Daniel.

"My dad uses this expression.

It came about in the early 19th century when boxing

rings were round. 

If anyone in the audience wanted to challenge a boxer,

he'd throw his hat in the ring."

"That's perfect," said Beth.

"Because you're going to get a challenge, running for

president against Paula!"

> **POP QUIZ**
>
> **Mark T for true or F for false.**
>
> In the early 19th century, boxing rings were square. T / F

KEY WORDS

- **mean** (mean-meant-meant)
- **be ready for**
- **expression**
- **come about** (come-came-come)
- **early**
- **century**
- **boxing**
- **if**
- **audience**
- **boxer**
- **perfect**
- **because**

Comprehension Quiz

A Match each character with the correct description.

❶   •   • a) Daniel's campaign manager

❷   •   • b) the quietest kid in the third grade

❸   •   • c) the most popular girl in the third grade

B Circle the right word for each underlined part.

❶ There were over (<u>one</u> / <u>two</u>) hundred students in the third grade.

❷ Daniel would need a majority of (<u>votes</u> / <u>buttons</u>) to win the election.

❸ Daniel already had the support of (<u>ten</u> / <u>two</u>) students.

C Mark T for true or F for false.

❶ Mr. Thomas supported Paula's plan 100 percent.　　T　F

❷ Daniel was ready for the challenge of running for president.　　T　F

❸ Daniel felt that he'd easily beat Paula in the election.　　T　F

D Choose the best answer to each question.

❶ Why did Beth want someone to run against Paula Stamp?

a) Beth thought Paula wasn't interested in being president.

b) Beth wanted one of her friends to be president.

c) Beth worried that Paula was too bossy.

d) Beth believed a boy would be a better president.

❷ Why were Daniel's friends surprised that he would run for president?

a) Daniel hated anything to do with government.

b) Daniel liked Paula Stamp and wouldn't want to beat her.

c) Daniel was the quietest kid in the whole third grade.

d) Daniel said he'd never run in an election at school.

Chapter Two

Finding a Winning Slogan

Beth flopped onto Daniel's couch and opened *The Essential Book of Presidential Trivia.*

"This book has everything we need!
We can check out all the slogans from presidential campaigns.
Maybe we'll get a few ideas."
Joey sat on one side of her and Daniel sat on the other side. **Aha!**

"Good thinking," said Daniel.

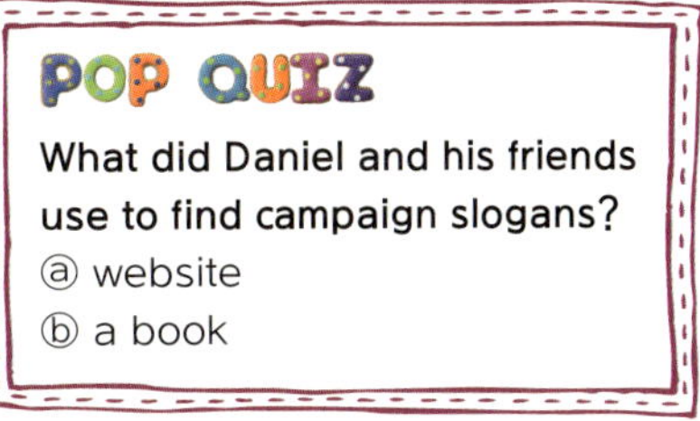

KEY WORDS

- **find** (find-found-found)
- **winning**
- **flop**
- **couch**
- **essential**
- **presidential**
- **trivia**
- **everything**
- **check out**
- **maybe**
- **a few**
- **side**
- **the other** (*cf.* other)
- **thinking**

"What was George Washington's slogan?" asked Joey.
"I'll bet he had a good one!"

"He didn't need one," said
Daniel.
"Washington was chosen by
the Electoral College." **Aha!**
"Yes," said Beth.
"He was chosen
unanimously, too.
That means everyone in the
Electoral College voted for
him."

▲ George Washington

KEY WORDS

- **I'll bet (that)** (*cf.* bet (bet-bet-bet))
- **be chosen** (*cf.* choose (choose-chose-chosen))
- **the Electoral College** (*cf.* electoral / college)
- **unanimously**
- **miss**
- **place**

- **process**
- **state**
- **certain**
- **elector**
- **Vice President** (*cf.* vice president)

"I think I missed the day we talked about that," said
Joey.

"Where's the Electoral College?"

"Well, it's not a place," said Daniel.

"It's a process.

Every state has a certain number of electors.

They vote for the President and the Vice President."

"Hold on," said Joey.

"I thought *we* vote for the President.

Well, I mean that our parents vote.

And anyone else who's a registered voter.

Isn't that right?"

"That's right," said Daniel.

"Voters go to the polls and fill out a ballot.

Most states have a 'winner takes all' system.
The candidate with the majority of the popular vote gets

all the electoral votes."

"And speaking of the popular vote…" Beth sighed.
"We're going to need a great slogan to beat the most
popular third grader!
She has a pretty terrific one."
Daniel gulped.
"What is it?"
"Go with a
champ and vote
for Paula Stamp,"
said Beth.
"Wow," said Daniel.
"That's really good.
Better start reading those slogans!"

KEY WORDS

- **Hold on!** (hold-held-held)
- **else**
- **registered**
- **voter**
- **poll**
- **fill out** (*cf.* fill)
- **ballot**
- **winner**
- **system**

- **candidate**
- **popular vote**
- **speaking of**
- **pretty**
- **terrific**
- **gulp**
- **champ** (= champion)
- **better**
- **read** (read-read-read)

Beth turned the page.

"The first slogan that helped to win an election was

▲ William Henry Harrison

'Tippecanoe and Tyler, too!' It was William Henry Harrison's slogan in 1840. **Aha!** He'd won a battle at a place called Tippecanoe, and John Tyler was his running mate. So that's how 'Tippecanoe and Tyler, too!' came about. Pretty catchy, huh?"

"I guess," said Joey.

"But Daniel hasn't exactly won any battles. And vice presidents in the school elections run on their own."

▲ a picture about the Battle of Tippecanoe

Daniel nodded.

"Did you know that the twins, Lucy and Luke Barkley, were running for vice president?"

"So either way, we're going to have a Barkley," said Joey.

"True, but all the girls will vote for Lucy," said Beth.

"There are more girls than boys in the third grade."

KEY WORDS

- first
- Tippecanoe
- battle
- running mate
- catchy

- huh
- guess
- not exactly
- any
- so

- either way (*cf.* way)
- more
- than

Vote Yourself a Farm!

"Instead of the two parties, the Republicans and the
Democrats, we have the girls versus the boys," said
Daniel.

"So it's just like you and Paula in the presidential
election.

We're going to need to get some girls on our side," said
Joey.

"Keep reading, Beth.

How about Abraham Lincoln?" (Aha!)

"Hmmm," she said.

"His slogan was, 'Vote Yourself a Farm.'"

"No," said Daniel.

"We need something more modern."

- instead of
- party
- the Republicans
- the Democrats
- versus

- keep + *Verb*-ing (keep-kept-kept)
- how about ~?
- farm
- modern (↔ old-fashioned)

▲ Calvin Coolidge

▲ Dwight Eisenhower

"Oh! Here's one that could've been written yesterday! It's for Calvin Coolidge: 'Keep Cool With Coolidge,'" said Beth. **Aha!**

"We could have 'Stay on the Sunny Side of the Street with Streeter!'"

Joey winced.

"No, thanks."

"I Like Ike?" asked Beth.

"That was for Dwight Eisenhower. I guess his nickname was Ike."

KEY WORDS

- **write** (write-wrote-written)
- **cool**
- **stay**
- sunny side
- wince
- Ike
- nickname

▲ Jimmy Carter
(By Unknown or not provided (U.S. National Archives and Records Administration) [Public domain], via Wikimedia Commons)

"Here's a funny one: 'Not Just Peanuts.' That was for Jimmy Carter." **Aha!**

"Well, he *was* a peanut farmer," said Joey.

"I think his other slogan was better, though," said Beth.

"A Leader, For a Change."

"Definitely better," said Joey.

"A leader…" said Daniel.

He snapped his fingers.

"Stand with a Leader!"

"Daniel Streeter!" said Beth and Joey.

KEY WORDS

- farmer
- though
- leader
- change
- definitely
- snap one's fingers
- real
- enough

Stand with a real leader, Daniel Streeter!

"I like it," said Daniel.

"Stand with a real leader, Daniel Streeter!"

It was a good slogan, he thought.

It might even be a great slogan.

But was it great enough to win over some of the third grade girls? **Aha!**

A Match each slogan with the right candidate.

❶ Abraham Lincoln   •   • a) "I Like Ike."

❷ Jimmy Carter   •   • b) "Keep Cool with Coolidge."

❸ Dwight Eisenhower •   • c) "Vote Yourself a Farm."

❹ Calvin Coolidge   •   • d) "Not Just Peanuts."

B Mark T for true or F for false.

❶ George Washington had a great slogan.   T F

❷ Washington was elected by Revolutionary soldiers.   T F

❸ The Electoral College is not a place.   T F

❹ Electors in the Electoral College have votes.   T F

❺ Daniel was sure his slogan would win lots of girl votes.   T F

❻ Daniel thought his slogan might be great.   T F

C Choose the best answer to each question.

❶ What did Beth bring to help with Daniel's campaign?

a) snacks

b) a new poster

c) a book of presidential trivia

d) glitter and construction paper

❷ Why was Paula Stamp's slogan so good?

a) It encouraged students to go with a champion.

b) It had lots of cheery colors.

c) It had extra-large letters.

d) It was just like a movie star's slogan.

❸ Why did Joey say that either way, a Barkley would be vice president?

a) Lucy Barkley was sure to win her race.

b) All the boys would vote for Luke Barkley.

c) The Barkleys are twins, and the only students running for vice president.

d) When a twin runs in an election, both of them win.

Chapter Three

The Rules of the Campaign

"Hurry," said Daniel.

"We can't be late to the meeting!"

Daniel and Joey pushed open the media center doors.

The room was filled with third, fourth, and fifth grade

students.

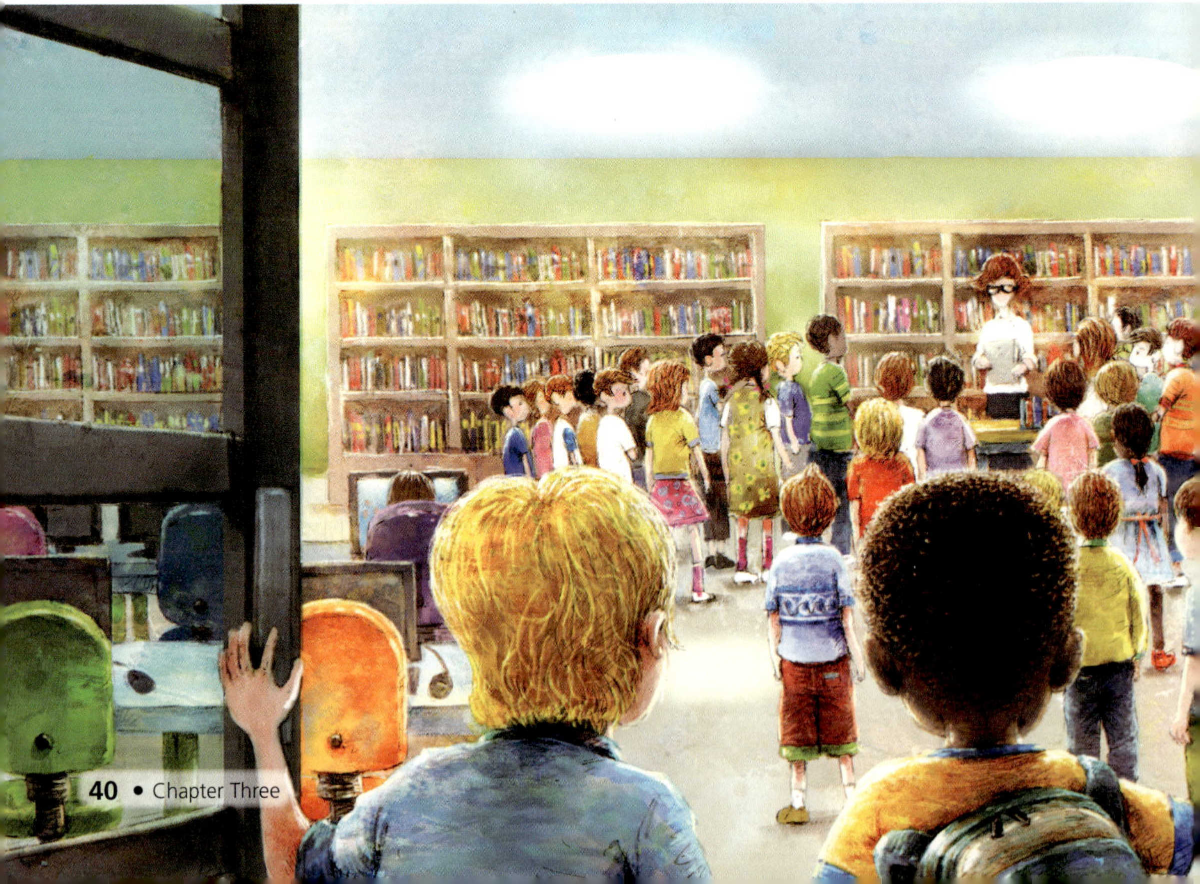

Those were the elementary classes that held elections.

Each grade would elect a president, a vice president, a secretary, and a treasurer.

All of them would be campaigning.

And every student who wanted to run had to follow the rules to the letter.

"Quiet, please," said the librarian, Mrs. Cooper.

She held a stack of papers.

"Please take a handout.

Keep the rules, but tear off the bottom part.

That's where you'll need to sign your name.

Then turn the form in."

Paula Stamp was the first to raise her hand.

"Mrs. Cooper, I don't think this is fair.

According to the rules, I can't give out candy."

"That's right," said the librarian.

"You cannot pass out candy or other materials to win a vote."

"But how are we supposed to get people to vote for us?" asked a girl in the back of the room.

KEY WORDS

- quiet
- librarian
- a stack of (*cf.* stack)
- handout
- tear off (tear-tore-torn)
- bottom
- sign
- turn in

- form
- raise
- according to
- give out (give-gave-given)
- pass out (*cf.* pass)
- material
- be supposed to + *Verb*
- back

Mrs. Cooper smiled.

"There are other ways to get votes," she said.

"You'll have your posters, and you can give out buttons, too."

"But we have to *make* the buttons."

It was Paula again, complaining.

▲ construction papers

"With construction paper that you provide. My mother was going to buy fancy buttons for me!"

"Not every candidate is able to buy buttons," said Mrs. Cooper. **Aha!**

"We want each candidate to have the same opportunity when it comes to campaigning."

"It's not like that in a *real* election," grumbled Paula.

- complain
- construction paper
- provide
- buy (buy-bought-bought)
- fancy
- be able to + *Verb*
- opportunity
- when it comes to
- grumble

A fifth grader raised his hand.

"Can we wear a T-shirt with our slogan on it?"

"Yes," said Mrs. Cooper.

"Use a solid colored T-shirt and make your own design.
Only the candidates and their campaign team can wear
special T-shirts.
You can't give them out to students."

- T-shirt
- solid
- own
- design
- only
- special

"Well, there goes another one of my ideas," said Paula.

"Honestly, I don't know why I'm even bothering to run."

"You can always drop out," said Joey. 

"And then my buddy, Daniel, would be our president."

Daniel smiled nervously.

"Oh, no, that's not going to happen," said Paula.

"I'll still win the election.

I've got an *amazing* speech!"

Daniel gulped.

He'd forgotten about the speech!

Every candidate had to give a speech.

Just thinking about standing in front of all those
students and talking made Daniel shudder.

Why had he said he'd run for president?

He felt sick to his stomach, listening to Mrs. Cooper.

KEY WORDS

- there goes
- another
- honestly
- bother
- always
- drop out

- and then
- buddy
- nervously
- happen
- amazing
- speech

- forget (forget-forgot-forgotten)
- give a speech
- in front of
- shudder
- feel sick to one's stomach
  (feel-felt-felt)(*cf.* stomach)

"Two minutes," she said.

"That's all the time you'll have on Monday morning.

You can use notes, but I recommend you memorize your speech.

It looks better when you're talking into the camera."

The camera!

Daniel almost laughed out loud.

He wouldn't have to stand up in front of the whole third grade class!

He only had to give his speech to the TV camera in the media center's studio.

He could do that!

Daniel signed the bottom of the form and placed it on Mrs. Cooper's desk.

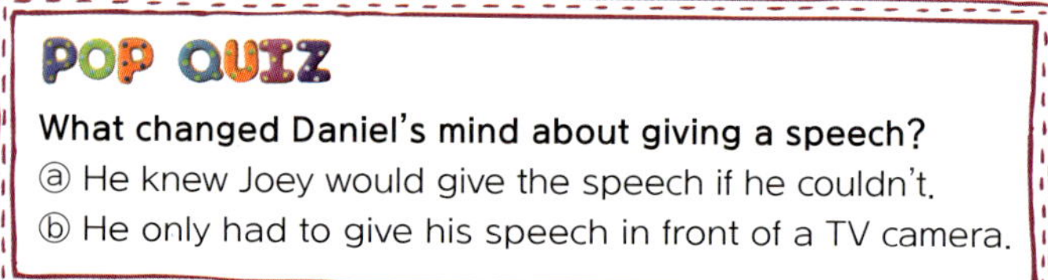

KEY WORDS

- minute
- note
- recommend

- memorize
- camera
- almost

- laugh out loud
- studio

"I'm so happy to see you here, Daniel," said Mrs.
Cooper.
"The third grade is going to have an interesting election,
I think."
She raised an eyebrow.
Daniel and Joey smiled.
"Just you wait and see," said Joey.
"Daniel's the man with a plan."
"Humph," said Paula.
"It's going to take more than a plan to beat *me*."
She placed her form on top of the stack.
"Make sure you follow all the rules, Daniel."
Then she secretly snatched Daniel's form from the pile.
Daniel turned and slung his backpack over his shoulder.
He didn't see his form, sticking out of Paula's back
pocket!

KEY WORDS

- **see** (see-saw-seen)
- **interesting**
- **wait**
- **humph**

- **on top of**
- **make sure**
- **secretly**
- **snatch**

- **pile**
- **sling** (sling-slung-slung)
- **backpack**
- **stick out of** (stick-stuck-stuck)

A Mark T for true or F for false.

❶ Only the students running for president were
allowed to campaign. T F

❷ Mrs. Cooper is Daniel and Joey's science teacher. T F

❸ Daniel and Joey attended a meeting about
election rules. T F

❹ Daniel was nervous when Mrs. Cooper mentioned
the speech. T F

❺ Only candidates running for president gave a speech. T F

B This is the process one must follow to run for president. Put the
sentences in order.

❶ Turn in the signed form.

❷ Pick up one of Mrs. Cooper's handouts.

❸ Tear off the bottom part of the form.

❹ Sign the bottom section of the form.

________ → ________ → ________ → ________

C Choose the best answer to each question.

❶ What advice did Mrs. Cooper give the students about making a speech?

a) Talk loud and look the audience in the eye.

b) Make sure to use words that everyone will understand.

c) Try to memorize the speech rather than reading it.

d) Don't worry about going over the time limit.

❷ Where was Daniel's permission form after the meeting?

a) on the bottom of the pile of forms

b) in the trash can

c) in Mrs. Cooper's desk drawer

d) in Paula Stamp's back pocket

D Circle the right word(s) for each underlined part.

❶ Daniel had better not read his (notes / slogan) during the speech.

❷ Daniel would give his speech to a (camera / tape recorder).

❸ Daniel was so relieved, he almost (cried / laughed).

❹ The studio was located in the (cafeteria / media center).

Chapter Four

Too Late
for Victory?

The next day, Beth, Daniel, and Joey stood patiently in line.

"I'd like 15 feet of brown, please," said Beth.

All the candidates were at the media center, getting their paper for posters.

Mrs. Cooper measured.

"That's a bit plain, isn't it?"

"Don't worry, Mrs. Cooper.

We have a great plan," said Beth.

"A terrific plan," said Joey.

"An out*stand*ing plan," said Daniel with a grin.

KEY WORDS

- **next day** (*cf.* next / day)
- **stand in line**
- **patiently**
- **would like** (*cf.* 'd)
- **feet** ($\fallingdotseq$ 30 cm)
- **measure**
- **a bit**
- **plain**
- **worry**
- **outstanding**
- **grin**

Mrs. Cooper paused.

"Daniel, I'm sorry."

She looked at a stack of forms on the desk.

"I can't give you any paper.

You didn't turn in your form."

"But I did turn it in," said Daniel.

"You saw me, Joey."

"Oh, that's too bad, Daniel," said Paula, standing behind him.

"I guess you won't be able to run for president after all."

"What?" Joey glared at Paula.

"That's not right.

He turned in his form!"

"Now, hold on a minute," said Mrs. Cooper.

"If you wait till I finish with everyone, we'll sort this out."

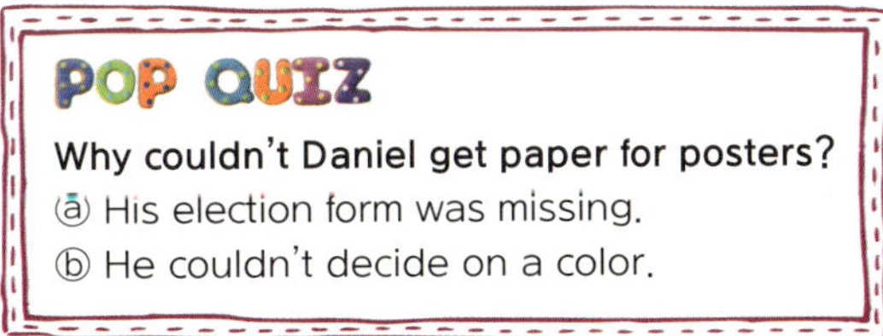

KEY WORDS

- pause
- sorry
- That's too bad.

- won't
- after all
- glare at

- till
- finish
- sort out

Daniel fumed as they waited at the end of the line.
By the time he filled out his form and got his materials,
the afternoon was almost gone.
Paula had already finished her posters and started on
her buttons!

Daniel sighed.
She had a great slogan, and the letters were practically perfect. They'd used a bucket of glitter, too. And her buttons were just as wonderful.

"She's got a big head start on us," said Daniel.

"You know we only have three days for campaigning!"

"Don't worry," said Beth.

"We'll catch up."

"I promise you," said Joey.

"We'll put up your posters today!

Then everybody will know who Daniel Streeter is!" **Aha!**

KEY WORDS

- **head start** (on)
- **catch up** (catch-caught-caught)
- **promise**
- **put up** (put-put-put)

Joey kept his promise.

They worked hard and Daniel had to admit that they'd done a great job.

After all, he had the only posters that hung vertically.

They had to hang upright because Beth had traced Daniel's body on the brown paper.

Then, they'd cut out his figure.

So students could actually stand next to a life-sized, paper Daniel Streeter!

- keep a promise
- hard
- do a job (do-did-done)
- hang (hang-hung-hung)
- vertically
- upright

- trace
- cut out (cut-cut-cut)
- figure
- actually
- next to
- life-sized

- hop off
- before
- hear (hear-heard-heard)
- hey
- outside
- recognize

The next morning, Daniel hopped off the bus.
But before he even walked into the school, he heard
someone call his name.

"Hey, look! It's Daniel Streeter!"

A boy stood outside the doors of the school.

How had he recognized Daniel?

Then Daniel remembered that he was wearing a T-shirt
with his slogan on it!

"It's about time you got here," said Joey, greeting him.

"Yes," said Beth, pulling Daniel into the school.

"Everyone is talking about your posters!"

A trio of third graders walked by.

"I'm voting for you, Daniel," said one of the boys.

"Me, too," said the other boy.

"Us guys have to stick together!"

"Thanks," said Daniel.

He turned to his friends.

"Do you really think they'll vote for me?"

"Sure," said Joey.

"I bet all the boys will vote for you!"

"But the girls," said Beth.

"Those votes are going to be much harder to win. **Aha!**

I hope you have a great speech."

Butterflies danced in Daniel's stomach.

He had the rest of the week to work on his speech.

For now, he and his campaign team needed to get his buttons finished.

Everywhere he looked, he saw Paula's campaign buttons glittering from third grade shirts!

KEY WORDS

- it's (about) time + *Subject + Simple Past Verb*
- greet
- pull
- trio
- walk by
- stick together
- harder
- butterfly
- dance
- rest
- work on
- for now
- everywhere

Lunchtime arrived and Daniel was even more worried.

He looked around at a sea of Paula buttons.

He tried to eat his sandwich, but it stuck in his throat.

Paula walked up to his table.

"Gosh, Daniel," she said.

"You must be the only third grader who's not wearing one of my buttons!"

She pulled a button from her backpack.

"Wouldn't you like one?" asked Paula.

"No, thanks," stammered Daniel.

It was almost true, he thought.

He and Joey and Beth were probably the only third graders not wearing a Paula Stamp button.

And it would be tomorrow before he passed out *his* buttons.

Would it be too late to stop Paula's runaway campaign? 

"Are you okay, buddy?" asked Joey.

"I'm fine," said Daniel.

But he couldn't swallow another bite.

POP QUIZ

Why did Daniel suddenly lose his appetite?
ⓐ He was nervous, seeing students wearing Paula buttons.
ⓑ He had already eaten too much peanut butter.

KEY WORDS

- lunchtime
- arrive
- worried
- try to + *Verb*
- eat (eat-ate-eaten)

- stick in
- walk up to
- gosh
- must + *Verb*
- No, thanks.

- stammer
- probably
- runaway
- fine

A Mark T for true or F for false.

❶ Joey saw Daniel turn in his permission form. T F

❷ Daniel's form was hidden on Mrs. Cooper's desk. T F

❸ Paula Stamp told Daniel he wouldn't be able to run for president. T F

❹ Daniel had to fill out the form again. T F

❺ Paula had finished her buttons when Daniel got his materials. T F

B Circle the right word for each underlined part.

❶ (Beth / Joey) told Daniel that everyone was talking about his posters.

❷ A trio of third graders is (two / three) people.

❸ A boy told Daniel that the guys had to (stick / laugh) together.

❹ Joey was sure that (all / some) of the boys would vote for Daniel.

C Choose the best answer to each question.

❶ What are the three things that made Paula's posters so wonderful?

a) extra-large size, bright color, and glitter

b) a great slogan, glitter, and the color blue

c) a great slogan, almost perfect letters, and glitter

d) perfect letters, a good slogan, and silver paint

❷ Why did Joey promise that everyone would know Daniel Streeter?

a) Joey was going to introduce Daniel to every third grader.

b) Joey planned to put an article in the newspaper.

c) Beth and Joey had a surprise banner made for Daniel.

d) The design of their poster would attract attention.

❸ How did a boy know Daniel when he hopped off the bus?

a) He'd seen the posters all over the school.

b) He was one of Daniel's good friends.

c) He saw Daniel's name on the T-shirt he was wearing.

d) Beth and Joey had pointed Daniel out to the boy.

Chapter Five

The Results Are in!

Monday had come all too soon for Daniel and his campaign team.

They'd given out all their buttons.

They'd asked every student in the third grade for a vote, even Paula Stamp.

Paula laughed.

"Sorry, Daniel, you won't get my vote," she said.

"I don't think you'll get *any* votes once the third graders hear my speech."

Daniel was afraid she was right.

The candidates had recorded their speeches just that morning.

It hadn't been easy for him, even though he only had to talk to a camera.

But Paula delivered her speech perfectly.

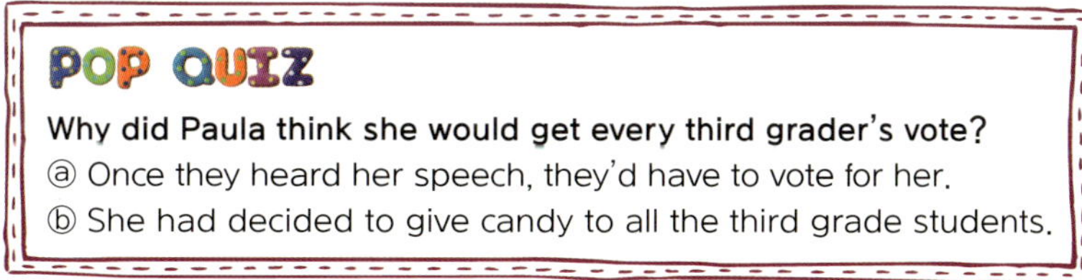

KEY WORDS

- result
- all too soon
- once
- afraid
- record
- easy
- even though
- deliver
- perfectly

The day passed in a blur, and at 2:15, the entire third grade gathered in the cafeteria.

Mrs. Cooper stood in front of a large screen.

"It's time to hear our candidates' speeches."

The students clapped.

Mrs. Cooper pointed to four tables.

On each table was a big box.

The box had a slot in the top.

"Those must be the ballot boxes," said Joey.

"Yes," said Mrs. Cooper.

"One for each class.

Don't forget to fill out your ballot!

The principal and I will tally the votes.

Candidates, please return at the end of the day for the

results."

Daniel squirmed.

Did he need to show up for the results?

Paula had a great speech!

Mrs. Cooper flipped a switch.

The screen lit up with the first candidate, a girl running for secretary.

Daniel tried to concentrate, but he kept thinking about his own speech.

Suddenly, Paula Stamp's face smiled at Daniel!

The presidential candidates were starting.

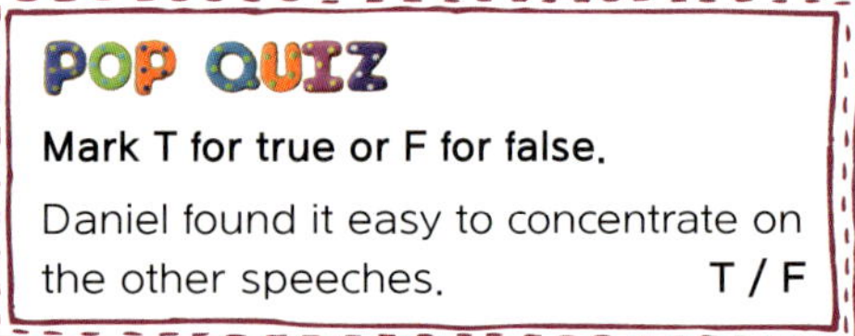

KEY WORDS

- squirm
- show up
- flip
- switch
- light up (light-lit-lit)
- concentrate
- suddenly

- pro (= professional)
- extra-large
- serve
- popcorn
- soft drink
- ring (ring-rang-rung)
- cheer (*cf.* cheering)

- finally
- fit
- period
- notice
- a lot of (= lots of)

Paula smiled into the camera, looking like a pro.

She promised extra-large ice cream bars every Friday.

She promised a movie night at the school, serving popcorn and soft drinks.

The cafeteria rang with cheers.

Finally, she promised that everyone would be more fit.

All they had to do was walk a mile during their lunch period.

Daniel noticed that there wasn't a lot of cheering for *that* promise.

In the next moment, Daniel's face filled the screen.

Could he win enough votes?

His speech didn't have all the bells and whistles like Paula's.

"G...g...good afternoon."

Daniel stuttered through his opening.

"I'd like to be your Third Grade P...President."

He cleared his throat.

He had a joke planned.

Would the students laugh?

"Even though a lot of you probably wondered if I could talk!"

Daniel heard a couple of kids laugh.

Whew, thought Daniel.

"I don't have a lot of big promises," said Daniel.

"But I have ideas.

First, I think managing the pencil dispenser should be a third grader's job.

I can fill up the pencil dispenser for the first month.

And then, other students can volunteer."

The boys cheered.

The pencil dispenser in the third grade hall had always been a fifth grader's job.

But most days, the dispenser was left empty when the fifth grader forgot.

It was so frustrating!

"I think walking is a good idea," said Daniel.

"But only if that's how you want to spend your time after lunch."

The boys cheered and a few girls cheered, too.

"We could have a Third Grade Walking Club for those who are interested.

And maybe some of you would like to talk about your favorite books.

We could have a Lunchtime Reading Club."

More students cheered.

"I can't promise extra-large ice cream bars or popcorn and movies," continued Daniel.

"And I'm not sure that *anyone* can keep promises like those.

But if I'm elected, I hope you'll come to me with *your* great ideas for the third grade.

And we'll try to make them happen.

That's a promise I *can* keep!"

Cheers erupted across the cafeteria.

Everyone was clapping!

Well, thought Daniel, everyone but Paula Stamp!

KEY WORDS

- **only if**
- **spend** (spend-spent-spent)
- **interested**
- **favorite**
- **continue**
- **erupt**
- **across**

Daniel
Stand with
a real leader,
Daniel Streeter!
Stand with
a real leader,
Daniel Streeter!

The late afternoon sun shone through the window in the media center.

Clumps of students sat at tables, waiting for the results.

Daniel and Joey waited at one table.

Paula and a few girls sat at a nearby table, laughing.

"You could pull off an upset victory," said Joey.

Daniel shrugged.

"Anything's possible, running for president."

Mrs. Cooper walked over and stood between the two tables.

"It was a very close vote," she said.

"And we counted twice, just to be sure."

Then she looked at Daniel.

Daniel nodded.

He was disappointed but he put out his hand.

"Congratulations, Paula."

"Oh, Daniel," said Mrs. Cooper.

She extended her hand.

"You're the new Third Grade President. Congratulations to *you*!"

Comprehension Quiz

A Mark T for true or F for false.

❶ Candidates should return the next day for the results. T F

❷ Daniel wasn't sure if he needed to show up for the results. T F

❸ The presidential candidates' speeches began with Paula Stamp. T F

B Circle the right word for each underlined part.

❶ When Daniel heard a couple of kids (laugh / cheer) at his joke, he felt better.

❷ Daniel did not make a lot of (promises / deals) in his speech.

❸ Daniel thought he could handle the (cost / responsibility) of refilling the pencil dispenser.

❹ The pencil dispenser in the third grade hall was a (fifth / third) grader's job.

 Choose the best answer to each question.

❶ Why did Daniel worry that he wouldn't get any votes?

a) The girls didn't like him.

b) Paula had given a better speech.

c) His buttons and posters weren't very appealing.

d) Paula Stamp told him so.

❷ What was a promise that Paula Stamp did NOT make?

a) extra-large ice cream bars on Friday

b) soft drinks and popcorn at a movie night

c) no homework on the weekend

d) a mile walk during the lunch break

❸ Why did Daniel think he'd lost the election?

a) Mrs. Cooper said it was a close election so he figured Paula won.

b) Mrs. Cooper looked at Paula Stamp and winked.

c) Daniel didn't think he got enough girl votes.

d) Daniel heard Paula laughing so he was sure she'd won.

Let's Review the Story

Fill in the blanks to review the story.

Title: Who'll Be __________ ?

Main Characters and Their Goals:

- Popular _______ Stamp wanted to be Third Grade President.
- Quiet _______ Streeter decided to run for Third Grade President.

The Obstacles that Daniel Faced:

- He is a quiet student so he was nervous about the election.
- He had to run against the most _______ girl in the third grade.
- He had to give a _______ to the entire third grade class.

The Ways in Which Daniel Overcame His Obstacles:

- He asked his _______ to help him with his campaign.
- He realized he only had to win a ma_______ of votes.
- He did not give up, even when Paula stole his permission _______ .
- He was able to r_______ his speech rather than speaking in front of the entire class.

The Factors That Led to Daniel Streeter's Win:

- His friends, _______ and B_______ , helped him.
- He had a creative sl_______ .
- He gave a fair and honest sp_______ .
- He never gave up.

Let's Think & Talk

Think about the following questions and answer them freely.

❶ Whose election slogans and promises do you think are better, Daniel's or Paula's? Why?

❷ Rearrange the election slogans of some former presidents of the United States. Which one do you think is best?

❸ If you were running for president, what slogan and election promises would you make for your election campaign?

Let's Review the Story

Title: Who'll Be **President** ?

Main Characters and Their Goals:

• Popular **Paula** Stamp wanted to be Third Grade President.
• Quiet **Daniel** Streeter decided to run for Third Grade President.

The Obstacles that Daniel Faced:

• He is a quiet student so he was nervous about the election.
• He had to run against the most **popular** girl in the third grade.
• He had to give a **speech** to the entire third grade class.

The Ways in Which Daniel Overcame His Obstacles:

• He asked his **friends** to help him with his campaign.
• He realized he only had to win a ma**jority** of votes.
• He did not give up, even when Paula stole his permission **form** .
• He was able to r**ecord** his speech rather than speaking in front of the entire class.

The Factors That Led to Daniel Streeter's Win:

• His friends, **Joey** and B**eth** , helped him.
• He had a creative sl**ogan** .
• He gave a fair and honest sp**eech** .
• He never gave up.

Go with a champ
and vote for
Paula Stamp!
Ne
she

Smart Readers: **Wise** & **Wide**

After-reading Test

- Who'll Be President?
- Level 3
- 26 Questions

  (Vocabulary 6 / Reading Comprehension 16/

  Sentence Structure & Grammar 4)

1. What does the word "majority" mean?
   ① more than half
   ② the least amount
   ③ exactly half
   ④ just a few

2. Which of the following is the opposite of the word "modern"?
   ① ugly
   ② old-fashioned
   ③ smart
   ④ historic

3. Which of the following is similar to the word "outstanding"?
   ① average
   ② silly
   ③ expensive
   ④ excellent

4. Which of the following has the wrong past tense form of the verb?
   ① beat − beat
   ② read − read
   ③ tear − tear
   ④ cut − cut

5. What is the right word for the blank?

> The school cafeteria buzzed ____________ news.

① in   ② to
③ off   ④ with

6. What is the common word for the two blanks?

> • Instead _________ the two parties, we have the girls versus the boys.
> • Just thinking about standing in front _________ all those students and talking made Daniel shudder.

① by   ② of
③ on   ④ to

7. Why would it take someone brave to run against Paula Stamp?
   ① Paula Stamp had a reputation for being mean.
   ② Paula Stamp wouldn't allow anyone to beat her.
   ③ Paula Stamp was the most popular girl in the third grade.
   ④ Paula Stamp was the biggest girl in the third grade.

8. Why did Beth agree to help Daniel in the election?
   ① She was sure Daniel could beat Paula Stamp.
   ② Daniel was one of her best friends.
   ③ She thought her teachers would give her extra credit.
   ④ She was very good at campaigning.

9. What three things did Beth think Daniel needed to run for president?
① bravery, honesty, and money
② posters, courage, and candy
③ posters, buttons, and a good slogan
④ time, money, and a good slogan

10. In the slogan, "Tippecanoe and Tyler, too," who was Tyler?
① the candidate running for President of the United States
② the running mate of William Henry Harrison
③ the campaign manager of George Washington
④ the brother of William Henry Harrison

11. Why was it necessary to have some girls on Daniel's side?
① The girls were the only ones who voted.
② There were more girls than boys in the third grade.
③ The boys were all voting for Paula Stamp.
④ The girls would help him campaign.

12. Which slogan gave Daniel a good idea?
① "Stay on the Sunny Side of the Street!"
② "A Leader, For a Change."
③ "Stand with Dan!"
④ "Vote Yourself a Farm."

13. Where were the student candidates scheduled to meet?
  ① in the cafeteria
  ② in the school principal's office
  ③ on the playground
  ④ in the media center

14. What was the first rule that Paula Stamp thought was unfair?
  ① Students were not allowed to give out candy.
  ② Students could not use purchased buttons.
  ③ Students were not allowed to use glitter on posters.
  ④ Students could wear specially printed T-shirts.

15. What was one of Mrs. Cooper's suggestions for getting votes?
  ① giving pencils to students
  ② promising to do students' homework for them
  ③ making and giving out buttons
  ④ sharing cupcakes with students

16. Why did Paula Stamp stay in the running for president?
  ① She wanted a new dress for when she won.
  ② She had an amazing speech.
  ③ She was sure her slogan was the best.
  ④ She had an amazing T-shirt design.

17. What was Mrs. Cooper worried about, with Daniel's posters?
   ① She didn't think he'd have enough paper.
   ② She thought his ideas were not very good.
   ③ She thought his choice of brown was too plain.
   ④ She didn't approve of his plans.

18. Why did Joey glare at Paula when Daniel's form was missing?
   ① He might guess that Paula had something to do with the missing form.
   ② Joey thought Paula's friends had taken the form.
   ③ Joey wanted to scare Paula so she'd quit the election.
   ④ He had something in his eye and it hurt.

19. What day of the week did students vote in the elections?
   ① Friday
   ② Monday
   ③ Wednesday
   ④ Saturday

20. How did Daniel know that one of Paula's promises was not very popular?
   ① The students cried.
   ② The students clapped loudly.
   ③ The students refused to listen.
   ④ The students did not cheer very much.

21. Why was the beginning of Daniel's speech funny?

    ① Daniel made a joke about stuttering.

    ② Daniel made fun of the other candidates.

    ③ Daniel made a joke about his quietness, how he didn't talk much.

    ④ Daniel made a joke about Paula Stamp's speech.

22. What was the one promise that Daniel made to the third graders?

    ① He promised a running club and a reading club.

    ② He promised that he would give the third graders regular ice cream.

    ③ He promised that he would listen to ideas and try to make them happen.

    ④ He promised that he would give a free pencil to each student.

※ Choose the wrong part of each sentence (23~25)

23. Those votes <u>are</u> going to <u>be</u> <u>many</u> harder <u>to win</u>.
            ①   ② ③   ④

24. But was <u>it</u> <u>enough great</u> to win over <u>some of</u> the <u>third</u> grade girls?
         ①   ②   ③   ④

25.

26. What is the correct sentence?

① But everyone call you Daniel, do they?
② But everyone calls you Daniel, didn't they?
③ But everyone calls you Daniel, don't they?
④ But everyone call you Daniel, don't they?

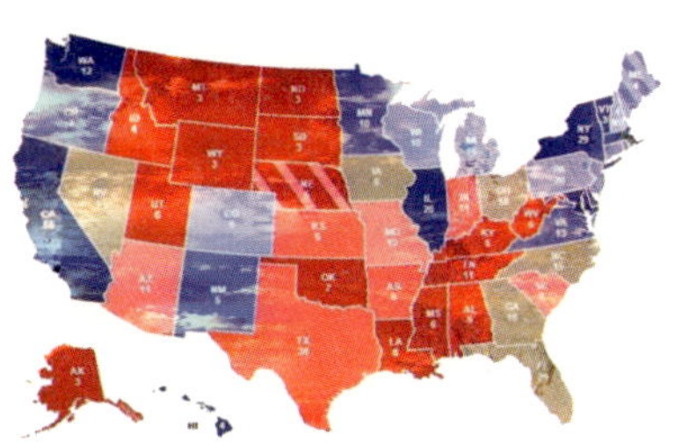

Cathy C. Hall
Cathy C. Hall graduated with a broadcasting degree, working in the radio industry as a news reporter and commercial copywriter before going back to school to earn English certification. She spent a decade in education, teaching preschoolers, middle schoolers, and high schoolers. Now, she's a full-time freelance writer, with stories, essays, and poems in publications for both children and adults. Her byline appears in books like *Uncle John's Facts To Annoy Your Teacher*, *Chicken Soup for the Soul's Think Positive for Kids*, *Cup of Comfort for Dog Lovers*, and many more.

 Smart Readers Wise & Wide **3-9**

Who'll Be President?

Written by Cathy C. Hall
Illustrated by Wookjae Lee

First Published in March 2017

Editorial Manager: Juyon Choi
Editors: Kyunghee Jang, Jiyeong Park
Designer: Eunhee Lee
Cover Designer: Eunhee Lee

Published and distributed by

 Happy House

Darakwon Bldg., 64-1 Jandari-ro, Mapo-gu, Seoul, Korea 04031
Tel: 82-2-736-2031(ext. 250)   Fax: 82-2-732-2037
Homepage: www.ihappyhouse.co.kr
Publisher: Kyudo Chung

ISBN: 978-89-6653-509-5 18740 / 978-89-6653-156-1 18740(set)

[Components]
- 1 Audio CD (Recording Studio: Aram)
- Answer Keys & Korean Translation: Free download at www.ihappyhouse.co.kr